'Tick, Tick, Tick' Says the Clock

Written By
Ngozi Elizabeth Mbonu

Illustrations By
Imashi Opatha

by Ngozi Elizabeth Mbonu

Copyright © Ngozi Elizabeth Mbonu 2024
First edition.

The right of Ngozi Elizabeth Mbonu to be identified as the sole author of this work has been asserted by her in accordance with the Copyright, Designs and Patterns Act 1988. Ngozi Elizabeth Mbonu is the sole author of this book.

All rights reserved. No part of this publication may be reproduced, stored in a retrieval system, or transmitted, in any form, or by any means (electronical, mechanical, photocopying, recording or otherwise) without prior written permission of the publisher.

The author Ngozi Elizabeth Mbonu will not be held responsible for any third parties, businesses or websites referred to in this book.

Although the author has made every effort to ensure that the information in this book was correct at press time, the author and publisher do not assume and hereby disclaim any liability to any party for any loss, damage, or disruption caused by errors or omissions, whether such errors or omissions result from negligence, accident, or any other cause.

ISBN **979-8-3335-1182-9**

Written by   **Ngozi Elizabeth Mbonu**
Illustrated by **Imashi Opatha** (comic.factory.productions@gmail.com)
Published by **CookieReads Publishing**

Printed & Published in Ontario, Canada

DEDICATED

TO

ALL THE YOUNG BOYS

AND

GIRLS IN THE WORLD

Tick! Tick! Tick!
Says the clock

What you have to do,
DO QUICK!

This book belongs to

....

"Tick, Tick, Tick"
Says the Clock

Written by
Ngozi Elizabeth Mbonu

They were supposed to be home by 5 o'clock; however,
    they played with their friends on the street for two hours and lost focus and track of time.

JAY:

"Please! Please! Can we quickly buy these few groceries? Our mom will be mad at us if we don't, and we have a long way to get home. Please help us, sir".

"No. The store is closed. Sorry. You'll have to come back tomorrow. Next time wear a watch".

The kids sigh and look at one another.
They start heading home;
running, skipping and laughing.

JAY:

"I think we better hurry home".

"Where are those kids! They've been gone for hours. Aha, there they are; afraid to come in!"

The next morning: "Wake up".

"I need to talk to you, and you all better listen carefully. I was very disappointed in you. When you are given something to do I trust you to be responsible and accountable for your actions.
 Yesterday, if you had been on time you would have had your favorite shepherd's pie not toast! I hope you have had time to think about what you did. Did you learn anything from your actions?"

Author

Ngozi Elizabeth Mbonu is the author of four Children's books titled *"Tatiana"*, *"Molly the best-behaved Student"*, *"Shine"*, *"Just like the birdies"*, *"Tick!Tick!Tick says the Clock"* and many more to come.

Ngozi Elizabeth Mbonu was born in Ottawa but spent most of her early years in West Africa.

She is a microbiologist, freelance photographer, entrepreneur who enjoys traveling and meeting people. In 2020 she moved to Kitchener, Ontario because of her love for nature.

"Tick!Tick!Tick says the clock" is her latest published children's book she hopes it's able to teach the importance of being on time, a good habit to master for a successful life. Her first book was turned into a movie by TIFF kids in Toronto; it addressed bullying amongst Kids. Her books have been reviewed by educators and added to library collections globally.

You can find her books on her websites
www.cookiereads.ca
She is also available on Amazon, Indigo and Walmart platforms.

Editor

Julie Thomas is a retired teacher of adult education in Toronto and a mentor to many. She loves reading, writing and spending time with her family.

Illustrator

Imashi Opatha is a freelance Artist cum Illustrator based in Sri Lanka. She is a Chartered Architect and later continued her higher studies at Post Graduate Institute of Archaeology in Sri Lanka. Her interest in Freehand drawing led into digital platform and now she is currently working as an online based Freelance Illustrator.

comic.factory.productions@gmail.com

Tick, Tick, Tick Says the Clock

Written By
Ngozi Elizabeth Mbonu

www.ingramcontent.com/pod-product-compliance
Lightning Source LLC
LaVergne TN
LVRC091352060526
838200LV00016B/368